21ST CENTURY WOMAN

From controlled to Freedom.

ROMIRA FRANCIS

Copyright © *Romira Francis*, 2024

All Rights Reserved

This book is subject to the condition that no part of this book is to be reproduced, transmitted in any form or means; electronic or mechanical, stored in a retrieval system, photocopied, recorded, scanned, or otherwise. Any of these actions require the proper written permission of the author.

Table of Contents

Chapter 1 The Drip Effect 1

    The Girl 2

    Love Bomb 3

    Rollercoaster 5

    Patterns 7

    The Ruins of Hope 9

    Dark Days 12

Chapter 2 Foul Play 14

    'Life Begins' 15

    Behind Those Eyes 17

    Leave Me Alone 19

    Go and Don't Look Back 21

    Spots Don't Change 23

    Puellae 26

    Not Again 28

    Never Again 31

Chapter 3 Innocents 34

    My Girls 35

    Me and You 38

    Baby Girl 40

Chapter 4 Take Flight 42

    You 43

    No More 45

    Now 47

    Panic 49

    Time to Let Go 52

    My Strength 55

The Right Choice 57

Chapter 5 Unchained **59**

    My Pain 60

    The Legislation 63

    Loneliness.. 65

    Nightmares.. 67

    It's my Turn 69

Chapter 6 A Certain Peace **71**

    Difficult Days 72

    Time Passes 74

    I am Finally Free 76

    Life is a Wonder 78

    Bluebirds 81

Chapter 1

The Drip Effect

The Girl

The girl never died,
She did not fade away,
The girl is blurry-eyed,
But she will always stay.
She is the strength within,
She directs my path,
She is in every cheeky grin,
She shares every bubble bath.
She shares my struggles,
She dances in my joy,
She is with me in my troubles,
She was never coy.
She never gave up a fight,
She helped carry the weight,
She was the light in the night,
She always believed in fate.
She is there in the music,
She is there when I dance,
She is there when I am sick,
She is there in every romance.
She is with me with my friends,
She will always be there,
Because she is me,
The girl within will live on.

Love Bomb

When we first met,
I was grieving for my son,
You said we could be a great duet,
You said I looked beautiful in the sun.

You promised me the best life,
You overwhelmed me with love,
You said you would save me from every low life,
You said everything I did you would be proud of.

You took me out for drinks and dinner,
You said you would give me everything,
You said I didn't need to be thinner,
You said you would be my king.

We did everything together,
Every day you made me smile,
You said you would protect me from every weather,
You were never ever hostile.

You spoiled me every day,
You said we were soulmates,
You said we would be together until we were old and grey,
You said our bright future awaits.

But then the mask started to slip,
I did everything I could to make it right,
Your behaviour got worse, you started to flip,
The sun no longer seemed so bright.

I could never have known what was to follow,
You didn't like me being away from you,
Your love started to feel hollow,
Then I started to feel blue.

I didn't expect the anger that came next,
I was inexperienced when it came to this,
Your moods became very complex,
I was no longer living in bliss.

Rollercoaster

It was you that was the lowlife,

I still didn't see this,

You are the one who caused strife,

You took away all of my bliss.

Your moods changed so quickly,

I couldn't keep up with it,

Your words started to become prickly,

But this you would not admit.

You then told me you were mentally unwell,

So, I got you the help you needed,

You still said you felt like hell,

So, I called the mental health team and pleaded.

This continued round and round,

From good days to the bad,

Then you pushed me to the ground,

You hurt me and made me feel sad.

You apologised and said it wouldn't happen again,

You started to cry and explain why,

Then you told me about all of your pain,

To make me believe you were not a bad guy.

You hugged me tight and said it would be alright,
You smiled at me instead of saying leave me be,
You started to turn back on the light,
Then carved our initials on a tree.

For several weeks I thought we were okay,
We went out to dinner and you held my hand,
I thought that maybe like this we would stay,
You said our lives you had already planned.

I spoke to a waiter to ask for some ice,
You seemed annoyed like I had done something wrong,
And then at the end I asked for the price,
Then we started to not get along.

Your mood switched again,
My head started spinning,
You started to cause me more pain,
But this was just the beginning.

Patterns

For several years the patterns repeated,
I still couldn't see that it wasn't me,
I felt like I had been defeated,
I didn't see that I needed to be free.

Again and again from heaven to hell,
Left me confused causing depression,
I couldn't take it when he would yell,
I didn't see I was just his obsession.

The cycle would start, tension building again,
Then would come an incident of his doing,
Somehow, I was always to blame,
Even though I could always feel it brewing.

Then came a sorry and the downplaying,
Again, we would go through the honeymoon phase,
I didn't see on me you were preying,
Your words you did cleverly phrase.

For years and years this went on,
The patterns repeating giving you the control,
I didn't see your love was a con,
I didn't know you had a goal.

Eventually you convinced me that I was the abuser,
I said I was sorry over and over,
You were always the accuser,
I didn't see it was a hostile takeover.

Saying I was sorry gave you more control,
Your behaviour got worse, you said it was my fault,
I started to see that you were the troll,
Then came the severe assault.

The Ruins of Hope

Her eyes inflated from the floods,

her heart aches from the loss,

her body feels lost &

her mind has shut down.

No more her mind screams,

no more her heart weeps,

no more her eyes beg,

no more her soul whispers, just no more.

No more risks to the heart,

no more open arms,

no more pain can she take,

no more she whispers, just no more.

The pain is deep,

no more guilt - let it go her soul begs.

She knows what she must do,

the path ahead is hard.

No more can she take watching people she loves in pain,

no more can she feel guilt and regret,

no more can her eyes continue to weep,

no more can she feel her heart break again and again watching people
she loves taken away.

Exhaustion levels are peaked,

mental capacity slows,

her skin feels sticky,

her eyes are swollen, tired and drained,

her soul wakes in tears each day,

her heart suffers the most.

No more midnight phone calls,

no more secrets shared,

no more can she miss them all every day,

no more talks about the weather in May,

for the memories are fading.

She is afraid of an empty future,

she is afraid of what lies ahead,

she is afraid to be alone, but she knows

she must walk through the fear to reach the other side.

No more will she let fear define her,

no more will she let her pain rule her life,

no more will she repeat past mistakes,

no more will she carry guilt and pain.

This she hopes is true,

this she will try to achieve.

When the clouds part and the sun shines through maybe then she can heal.

Until then,

no more are the words echoing,

no more ....

Dark Days

Today the dark clouds keep going,
today the tears keep flowing,
today my mind keeps blowing,
today my anxiety keeps growing.

No one can hear me crying,
no one can hear me shout,
no one can see me waving,
no one knows I'm about.

I'm alone in my darkness,
I'm alone in my torture,
I'm alone in my sadness,
I'm alone in my future.

Today was harder than yesterday,
today I faced my fears,
today I broke my own heart,
today brought me to tears.

Nobody can feel the sharp breaths,
nobody can feel the pain,
nobody can feel the burning eyes,
nobody can feel them,

because they are mine.

All alone in my sorrow,
all alone in my room,
all alone in Chicago,
all alone in my home.

Today was a bad day,
today hurt my head,
today I lay in my nightmares,
today I lay in my bed.

Maybe tomorrow will be different,
maybe tomorrow I will find peace,
maybe tomorrow this will be a dream,
maybe tomorrow I will find another puzzle piece.

Maybe just for one day,
or even just an hour,
please grant me my wish,
for I am losing power.

Chapter 2

Foul Play

'Life Begins'

Take the medication they said,

It will help they said,

You will feel better before you know it.

The side effects kick in,

The anxiety builds,

I feel like crawling out of my skin,

this doesn't feel like a rebuild.

The tears start to flow,

the pain is immense,

my thought pattern isn't slow,

I am still on the fence.

I want to throw them in the bin,

I want the effects to begin,

how can they work when I feel like this,

how can they know I just want bliss.

I stayed firm and didn't give up,

for this has been a long build-up,

I started to feel the fog fading,

as the tears stopped cascading.

The sun had started to shine,

I started to clear the shrine,

I remembered how to smile

for this had been gone awhile.

The pit of my stomach stops shaking,

I even started baking,

the crease between my brow had gone,

these pills are no con.

I can now breathe each day,

and even plan for May,

I am really glad I took them,

my life wouldn't be the same without them.

I can live my life now,

this is where my life begins..........

Behind Those Eyes

When I know someone well,
And I've seen behind those eyes,
I do not need to dwell,
On the pretences and hidden lies.

I started to see the patterns,
And all his clever tricks,
He never learns, I still have concerns,
There was never a quick fix.

Honesty isn't in his vocabulary,
He needs a better dictionary,
Is all this drama really necessary,
Everything he says is imaginary.

I cannot stress this enough,
He really has to go,
Life shouldn't be this tough,
It's time to breathe and grow.

He held me back for so long,
Now he gives me no choice,
I will express it in a poem or a song,
I know I will find my voice.

I have so much to live for,

So much to still learn,

Maybe buy new decor,

And live with less concern.

I cannot do this until he is gone,

And I'm released from his tight hold,

Life has felt like a marathon,

Now, I'm taking off my blindfold.

This is not up for discussion,

I don't want to hear him explain.

He will get his repercussion,

He will not hurt me again.

Leave Me Alone

When will you just leave me alone,
When will you learn that no is no,
When will you see that I have grown,
I will no longer go with your flow.

You will never get your own way,
I will fight you on this each and every day,
My children are not here for you to abuse,
You have always had such a short fuse.

Those fake tears don't work with me,
So why won't you just leave me be,
Nobody will believe your lies,
All I did was try and compromise.

You are so full of excuses,
You caused us all psychological bruises,
You are a sorry excuse for a man,
We will not follow your plan.

I will protect us from you,
All you do is cause us to feel blue,
No more confusion and tears,
No more sending them upstairs.

All you do is try to control,

This time, you will get more than parole,

I have been digging myself out of a hole,

You don't know that I have a goal.

Go and Don't Look Back

Don't you see, you have no chance,
Everyone else, can see it at a glance,
You previously had me in a trance,
Purely because of circumstance.

I know I could never love you again,
My god, you are so very vain,
Put away your chain and just refrain,
Make my day and get on a plane.

Why is no never enough,
Why is everything with you so tough,
Living life with you is so damn rough,
Go back inside and remove your stuff.

You always think you are in the right,
Living life like it's a constant fight,
Always holding on to me too tight,
While living in a total bombsite.

You always did want to upstage,
Never wanted to talk or engage,
Always on a reckless rampage,
Locking me up tight in a cage.

I will not live my life like this,
No, no, I don't want a kiss,
I definitely don't want to reminisce,
This isn't living life in bliss.

Go out that door and don't come back,
Don't forget that other backpack,
Go and drive off in your hatchback
My footsteps, you can now never track.

Spots Don't Change

You said I could trust you,
You said you had changed,
The lies I can see right through,
You had just rearranged.

You filled my head with information,
You lied and you lied,
You had no hesitation,
You don't know, I am now wide-eyed.

For every word that you speak,
I expect it to be a lie,
Your narcissistic techniques,
I am not yours to buy.

The emotional manipulation,
In everything you have and will say,
Just like a rat is to a Dalmatian,
You just see me as easy prey.

Your tricks that used to work,
Twisted to look honest,
I can still see your hidden smirk,
Your eyes still so dishonest.

You can never know me,

All you see, is you,

Even down in one knee,

Nothing about you is true.

You think poems and flowers will work,

I know this trick the most,

You plan to build me up like brickwork,

But in the end, I know what this will cost.

The only goal you have is control,

Step back, see you have lost,

I know you have no soul,

Your heart will never defrost.

I have strength within me,

You never saw,

It's time for you to flee,

Before my horde knock down your door.

I have strength I had to find,

While I lied awake at midnight,

You made a mistake, you thought I was blind,

You have no idea, I now have foresight.

Every action has an ulterior motive,
Every tear has a purpose,
From an outside perspective,
You only ever wanted to destroy us.

I only ever wanted to feel bright,
I wanted to fight for my dream,
You only ever wanted to fight,
We were never on the same team.

Your alibis are not airtight,
You cannot reach my height,
I know I will be alright,
I don't have to live in fight or flight.

You will never change your spots,
Your voice leaves my stomach in knots,
A dread feeling from within,
I must lift up my chin.

You will never win,
I have what I need,
Now my life can begin,
For I can now be freed.

Puellae

How could you do that to them,

After everything you went through,

Everything with you is mayhem,

You keep leaving them feeling blue.

You have a short temper,

This is well known,

From shouting to a whisper,

Aggression and a groan.

You could have been their hero,

But that was never you,

You vote for the anti-hero,

This I always knew.

I did not see the severity,

In everything that you do,

You think you are the almighty,

Everyone else is under your shoe.

You shout and you push,

You name call and abuse,

Sometimes you smush,

And then you accuse.

You try to control them,

Instead of guiding them,

You can't see the damage you've done,

This did not stop at just one.

It seems we have all had a turn,

To experience your evil,

All you have is self-concern,

Everything with you is medieval.

So now I must keep them safe,

With everything in my power,

They shouldn't feel unsafe,

Or feel the need to cower.

I will teach them right from wrong,

And help them heal from you,

Maybe turn this into a song,

Their lives will feel brand-new.

I know now what I have to do,

To protect my babies from you,

I will leave all of my belongings behind,

And take them somewhere you can't find.

Not Again

I told myself it would be fine,
I could handle this, stay in control,
I thought I knew every sign,
He could not get me back in that hole.

He said that he would behave,
And behave he mostly did,
I thought that I could be brave,
Until he took off that lid.

It was slowly at first,
Like the rain when it spits,
I didn't see I was being coerced,
He got in all his first hits.

Controlling my behaviour,
My actions and money,
Saying he is my saviour,
And as soft as a bunny.

These eyes aren't blind,
Emotions in a wreck,
Never giving me peace of mind,
In chess, this is check.

Time goes by, I am fed lies,
Chest pains are building, it's him I despise,
From the outside I know what to advise,
All I see in him, are snake eyes.

He always was creative,
Said he would do anything,
He uses his creativeness to be deceitful, manipulative,
narcissistic and controlling, he's always in a mess.

Why is he so obsessive,
Why won't he let me go,
Why is he so possessive,
I feel like I need ammo.

I need a security blanket,
Or a new hidden nest,
Pass me another cigarette,
The next bit's the best.

He thinks he has won,
Ducks lined up in a row,
He has had his fun.
And made it to the end of the rainbow.

There is one thing he doesn't know,
Is how much the abuse can really show,
On this I will be careful and slow,
All the while pretending to glow.

I have hidden support,
This I do not report,
I will take him to court,
On this I will not abort.

When I am free, I will jump for joy,
Free to be me, away from the boy,
For now, I must flee,
To be, just us three.

Never Again

Why would you think I would give in to you,
After everything you went and put us through.
You lie, you manipulate, you speak out of turn.
You're a mess at your best and you never learn.
You play your games and you think I'm blind,
So, I've made up a rhythm for you to find.
You think I'm a fool,
I will take you to school,
I don't follow your rules,
I have a fabulous new tool.
You treated me badly,
Most of it verbally,
Your clever tricks,
And the pain it inflicts,
Your arrogant thinking,
And all of your bamboozling,
Your attitude is stinking,
But I've been busy linking.
I broke free from the opposite of a dream,
I no longer want to cry and scream,
we were never really on the same team,
You took everything to the very extreme.
Life with you was always hell,

Like living in a damp cold cell,

I now enjoy a clean quiet hotel,

After I chose to say farewell.

So why would you think I would give in to you,

When you make me feel so terribly blue.

My home no longer includes you,

There will never be a new review.

My only regret is I didn't leave sooner,

I should have believed every tiny rumour,

That you are a schmoozer and a user,

A nasty bully and an abuser,

You always thought you could be a ruler,

As you thought about every tiny manoeuvre.

Your biggest mistake was picking me,

Look at me now for I am free,

The one thing I want to make quite clear,

I know everything you say is insincere,

You only want to install insecurities and fear,

And continue to whisper bad things in my ear.

I will tell you something I certainly know,

Our love is as dead as Marilyn Monroe.

Our story has ended,

Trying is not recommended,

This princess is now defended,

With everything life intended.

I am not yours to keep, borrow or control,

I know how you like to tear at my soul,

You always left me with a great big hole but now I just feel content and whole.

There was a strength within me that I had to find,

My mind is clear and redefined,

Now I know how to calm and unwind,

You will always and forever be declined.

Chapter 3

Innocents

My Girls

No matter what, I will be here for you,
I will not watch others make you feel blue,
I will teach you right from wrong,
I will show you how to be headstrong.

I'm sorry it took me so long,
To show you how to be strong,
Everyone experiences pain,
But history doesn't need to repeat again.

I will help you learn,
Why we can't return,
To someone who can treat you badly,
Even if you love them madly.

Love isn't always enough,
When the one you love,
Always makes life so tough,
Always wearing a boxing glove.

I'm so sorry you feel pain,
Let's get away on a train,
Somewhere we can be happy and heal,
I know this is a rubbish deal.

Home isn't where our things lay,

Homes is where we are,

It's wherever we stay,

We will be happier by far.

I'm hoping you won't hate me,

I will explain why we had to flee,

We will be happier just us three,

Maybe we can go on a shopping spree.

Now we can sing and dance,

Not living life in a trance,

I wish I could have told you in advance,

But I couldn't under the circumstance.

I love you both more than words can explain

I will always run with you in the rain,

I will be your Mum and Dad,

The best anyone has ever had.

We can watch a movie,

While we drink a smoothie,

We can have sleepovers,

You won't need to eat the leftovers.

You both deserve so much more,
Than only seeing me from the door,
I would never favouritise either of you,
We have to stick together like glue.

I am now breaking the chain,
I know I must not refrain,
I have to relieve this chest pain,
My freedom I will regain.

You are both so beautiful and kind,
I do not want you to be defined,
By the cruelty and abuse,
For which there is no excuse.

Me and You

I'm sorry I couldn't stop it,
I'm sorry I didn't run away,
I'm sorry you felt like a misfit,
I will be sorry every day.

This poem is for you,
My first-born beautiful girl,
I've finally had a breakthrough,
You were always my super girl.

I can see the toll it has taken,
The weight and the exhaustion,
Hunny it's time to reawaken,
You are not godforsaken.

You didn't deserve the hell you went through,
Someone please pass me the tissue,
I feel so much pain inside,
That I always had to hide.

I never wanted that life for you,
I never wanted you to feel so blue,
Now you need a medical mental health crew,
Because he put us under his shoe.

I'm sorry for everything you saw,
I'm sorry for every time I didn't draw,
I'm sorry I was sometimes distant,
Or if I was ever inconsistent.

You have always been so brave,
It wasn't your fault you would misbehave,
You had internal struggles and fear,
I always tried to help my dear.

I know you have residual pain,
He really did mess with your brain,
I understand forgiveness isn't always easy,
But we never had it light and breezy.

I will help you heal and help you regain,
The freedom you lost and scars from the pain.

Baby Girl

I'm so sorry I'm not there for you,
I'm so sorry you don't understand,
I'm so sorry that you feel so blue,
I'm so sorry this had to be planned.

I miss you every day,
Seeing you so sad breaks my heart,
I miss the times that we play,
It pierces my heart like a dart.

Lift up your chin blue eyes,
This won't be forever,
Maybe we can watch the butterflies,
You are so very beautiful and clever.

Dry those eyes baby girl,
Nanny will always be here for you,
Maybe we can twirl and whirl,
Then you can help me make a stew.

I know things are tough right now,
And you are struggling to cope deep down,
Maybe if life will allow,
You can come and stay, lift up that brow.

Until then you can see me on the phone,

    I will try and make you smile,

    You never have to feel alone,

    This is only for a little while.

Chapter 4
Take Flight

You

It was a choice I had to make,
Everything about you was fake,
All you ever did was cause me heartache,
This would leave me with a constant headache.

Now I realise that it wasn't heartbreak,
You would always cause a mighty earthquake,
You threw me around causing backache,
Calling me names like stupid and snowflake.

All you did was take and take,
Leaving me afraid, lying wide-awake,
There was never any give and take,
I felt like I needed an emergency brake.

I just wanted to have a coffee break,
But you decided that you wanted steak,
Screaming at me until I had earache,
When I needed to sleep, you would keep me awake.

No, I don't want your gifts as a keepsake,
You were awful when it was time to wake,
On birthdays and holidays you were a flake,
Your mood swings left me with bellyache.

Hearing your voice makes me shake,
I should have seen that you were a snake,
I'm lucky I didn't end up in the bottom of a lake,
Now you are my past and my biggest mistake.

No More

No more pain and constant confusion,
No more being mistreated by you,
I have now come to the conclusion,
That it was always you, this is a breakthrough.

You blamed me for your mistakes,
Convinced me that I should hate myself,
That I was the one causing the headaches,
That I caused you to want to hurt yourself.

I now know this was your manipulation,
Every word you said was to gain control of me,
You twisted the truth so I would lose concentration,
Now I can be happy and carefree.

You didn't see it coming,
We were there, then we weren't,
You didn't know we would go running,
I did warn you I was now different.

The change in me took many lessons,
Right in front of you but you were blind,
I attended many, many sessions,
With research and the course combined.

My eyes were opened to your ways,
This gave me freedom from your lies,
The help I received I will always praise,
To many other women, I can now advise.

The domestic abuse course,
And the national helpline,
They are a great source,
They really are divine.

The refuge saved our lives,
The staff are so wonderful,
No more words that feel like sharp knives,
Now everything just feels colourful.

Now

What game are you playing now,

Trying to make contact any way you can,

I just look and raise an eyebrow,

You are nothing more than a conman.

My girls are safe and happy with me,

We do not need bitter words and greed,

So go away and leave us be,

Without you we will be sure to succeed.

Life with you was like hell on earth,

Stuck in a cloud of your dark words,

Now I really know my worth,

We will fly away like mockingbirds.

No more worrying about your next mood swing,

Never again will I feel my back hit the stair,

I'm now looking forward to what the future will bring.

To be free from you is like a breath of fresh air.

I can now process what you put us through,

The pain, the tears, evil words and manipulation,

For never have I known someone as evil as you,

I now feel like I'm on permanent vacation.

Life from now on will be so much simpler,
Breathing and speaking is no longer hard,
I will never be with anyone even slightly similar,
I will not live a life always on guard.

Panic

Just as I think I have found peace,

You find another way to get at me,

This just causes the panic to increase,

Just when I'm trying to pick up the debris.

Your Mum isn't much better,

She prods and pokes for information,

Then you send me that letter,

Because you both want to know our location.

The anxiety started to build within,

I felt sick, my head started to spin,

I know you are just trying to win,

And do anything you can to get under my skin.

My legs started to tremble,

My body covered in sweat,

My emotions I wanted to disable,

This all felt like another threat.

My chest started to feel tighter,

It felt like it would lead to my death,

I know at heart I am a fighter,

But it felt like I was out of breath.

My vision became blurry,
I was suddenly very dizzy,
I felt like I needed to hurry,
I knew that I was very busy.

Eventually I had to stop,
And breathe in and out slowly,
Before I could go to the shop,
I felt like I looked very lowly.

Eventually I felt like I could breathe again,
My body began to stop shaking,
I could no longer feel the chest pain,
My body was left with aching.

I know why this has happened,
I know that I will get past this,
I don't need to feel saddened,
My feelings I cannot dismiss.

I will work on how I'm feeling,
I will process what you did to me,
The panic is very revealing,
I know most people will agree.

One day I will be free of this,
And the repercussions of your abuse,
One day I will feel bliss,
And be able to let loose.

Time to Let Go

How dare you say those things about me,
And make me out to be the bad one in this,
Lies to you are like pollen is to a bee,
But everything you say I will just dismiss.

Call me names, say I did this and that,
At the end of the day, you still have to live with you,
Go on, put on your face paint and your hat,
They will say your name, I will say who.

You no longer have a place in our lives,
You will have to live with all your lies,
You can play with your bat and your knives,
But the truth is always in your eyes.

So stop and think before you shame my name,
The more you push, the worse you look,
They all know I am not to blame,
This will all go into my book.

I should have known better when I first met you,
It was always about you and how you felt blue,
I was always trying to help you get through,
When you were stuck in a queue or said you had the flu.

Fifteen years on and now I know better,
I hear your lies and see your games,
And every manipulation in every letter,
Now I want to see them go up in flames.

Don't blame me for your mistakes,
I know each and every little game you play,
Every word you say, leaves me with the shakes,
You will still be this way when you are old and grey.

So go ahead and play your mind games,
They don't work on me anymore,
Go ahead and make your claims,
Everyone can now see who you are at your core.

Nothing you can do will shock me,
I don't need anyone to be happy,
I am sure that the courts will agree,
Especially when they see you get snappy.

Our children are better off without you,
The older they got, the worse you became,
You didn't like the fact that they grew,
To see everything with you is just a game.

No court will force them to see you,
Especially when they see the video of your abuse,
You are better off living in a zoo,
We all know you will just take to the booze.

We will get on with our lives,
To be free of you and start again,
We can grow fruit, vegetables and chives,
Without you there to complain.

My Strength

I will remember who I am,
I will fight for justice,
All your crap will drop into my spam,
I will never look back at what was us.

You are a sorry excuse for a man,
All you did was point out my flaws,
Maybe you think you have a plan,
But you haven't researched the laws.

No matter what you do,
You will not win this war,
Because nothing you say is true,
So go back to your dirty floor.

I will find my strength again,
You can never break me for good,
It's your turn to feel the pain,
Because you never thought I would.

Your words no longer scare me,
I have the back-up and witnesses, not you,
You will no longer be able to use your key,
It's time you know what it's like to feel blue.

I will get stronger every day,
No one will break me again that way,
Now I can dance and enjoy reggae,
Without being told that I am gay.

I will be the strongest woman anyone could meet,
The pain and the trauma will not define me,
I know how to stand on my own two feet,
I will learn to be me and forever feel free.

You will never get your own way again,
I will make sure of that,
Now I can go where I want on a plane,
It's time for you to get out of my flat.

You think holding my things hostage will get a response,
You are very wrong as I know your game,
Do you really think that I am that dunce,
The more I think about it, you really are that lame.

I will move on and never look back,
You will be stuck in your own trap,
My footsteps you will never track,
You will never make me snap.

The Right Choice

I have earned the right to find my peace,

And the right to put my life back together piece by piece,

I have earned the right to protect myself,

I have earned the right to put my life back on the shelf.

You have no right to judge me,

The right thing was to flee,

It doesn't matter if you don't agree,

We have a right to be free.

The pain in which he inflicted,

Should get him convicted,

This was all self-inflicted,

Our lives should not be restricted.

The panic I lived with every day,

The breathes he restricted from my airway,

I did not want him to stay,

But stay he did anyway.

He only cares for number one,

I did not see or feel the sun,

He left me no choice but to run,

After he thought he had won.

Why can't you open your eyes and see,
That he abused them and me,
None of us should ever have to plea,
We should be able to live our lives carefree.

Nobody should have to feel afraid,
Holding back the tears so they don't cascade,
At home the evil in him was displayed,
Turning me, into his daily maid.

We shouldn't be his punching bag,
Or feel like we are wearing a dog tag,
We shouldn't have to wear a gag,
Because at home he waved his red flag.

Chapter 5

Unchained

My Pain

Why were you so obtuse,
You were meant to be a loved one,
All of the nightmares about your abuse,
PTSD really isn't fun.

I still have to deal with the mess you made,
My confidence you destroyed,
The money you took, when I was paid,
And the bad memories I try to avoid.

The flashbacks keep coming,
Your hands around my neck,
Treating me like your plaything,
Always leaving me in a wreck.

The awful words you used,
The names you always called me,
You wanted me to be confused,
Never knowing how to be free.

You threw me around like a raggy doll,
Smashing me against the wall,
It was fear you wanted to install,
Always behaving like Mr know-it-all.

I now struggle if someone shouts,
Anxiety builds and my head starts to hurt,
Leaving me with many doubts,
So I just want to crawl into my nightshirt.

The memories of you screaming in my face,
Worried I may end up in a briefcase,
Never giving me any headspace,
A knife under my mattress just in case.

My children needed me to be around,
So I grinned and bared everything you did,
Even when you threw me on the ground,
The cuts and bruises I always hid.

I don't know why I didn't leave sooner,
The trauma you caused prevented that,
You then started doing it to her,
Treating her like a doormat.

You had done this before,
I did everything to help but leave,
You said never again and this you swore,
I know that I was just naive.

Now we are safe and hidden away from you,

I know this is a much better deal,

We can start to heal and feel brand new,

Now I am the only one behind the wheel.

The Legislation

You always thought you were a great debater,
Now I can see you are just a dictator,
A hater causing holes like the equator,
With sharp teeth like an alligator.

You always thought you were a Gladiator,
I know you to be a fabricator,
Always trying to be the navigator,
Never listening to the operator.

I will not be your collaborator,
I have always had to be the communicator,
You were always the interrogator,
And the evil manipulator.

I had to become the negotiator,
And eventually the investigator,
While you became the prosecutor,
And the common denominator.

I had to become the speculator,
And the administrator,
You became the terminator,
While I lived on a metaphoric ventilator.

All I needed was a vindicator,

Yet you were just a violator,

We do not need a mediator,

You can live alone in your simulator.

Loneliness

Sometimes I feel so deeply alone,
But I just keep going,
My future is always unknown,
But I must keep growing.

Each day comes and passes me by,
I do the chores and dinner each night,
sometimes I look at the sky and sigh,
Sometimes I feel I still have to fight.

Some days I'm happy and I smile,
Some days my emotions are under control,
No one around me is being hostile,
And every laugh soothes my soul.

But then come the days where the tears keep flowing,
All of my emotions start overflowing,
I know I must stay strong and keep going,
Even when I don't feel like being outgoing.

The pain comes and runs me over,
I feel lonely deep in my soul,
I just want to lay in my bedcover,
What's the point in this birth control.

This isn't how my life was meant to be,

Is the thoughts ringing in my head,

My life was supposed to be full of glee,

Not full of pain and bloodshed.

Maybe this is the curse of the ADHD,

To feel everything so very deeply,

To struggle not to go on a shopping spree,

And to feel like I've been treated so cheaply.

I'm not looking for Prince Charming,

I enjoy my peace and making my own decisions,

I find some people's behaviours very alarming,

Maybe I just need better provisions.

Nightmares

Nightmares, nightmares,

Please go away,

Always leaving me in tears,

It's like a pirouette in ballet.

Round and round I go,

There's no end in sight,

Nightmares on overflow,

Dreams full of fight of flight.

When will these dreams leave me alone,

When will I be healed with no overflow,

It feels this is very unknown,

Buried deep as if under thick snow.

Nightmares, nightmares,

Please just stop,

I am making mental repairs,

So, I can feel on top.

Dreams were satan still attends,

A place where he can still obsess.

A merry-go-round that never ends,

My nerves are still a mess.

One day these dreams will go away,

One day I will be free,

One day it will be the past and I pray,

One day my dreams will just be me.

It's my Turn

You believe you are an alpha male,
But really you are just a boy,
I know what you'll be thinking when make bail,
Every thought will be to destroy.

I will show you what I'm made of,
I won't stop until I get justice,
Go ahead, put on your boxing glove,
You won't reach me through the abyss.

You put me down, you called me names,
You shoved me around like your plaything,
I can't count all of your manipulative games,
This time I have told them everything.

I will fight back, use everything I can,
I won't stand back and let you walk all over me,
Boy, you better believe I have a plan,
I know this time; I will stay free.

You think you can take my children from me,
Think again, I will fight to the end,
It wasn't just me that needed to flee,
Show your real face, we know you just pretend.

The people that matter; have my back,
You can try to drag me through the ringer,
But you are the one that will receive the blowback,
This is not a late-night show on Jerry Springer.

No matter what tactic you try,
You are just hiding behind that fake smile,
You have always been such a bad guy,
You are exiled, we know you are vile.

Even if they don't lock you up behind bars,
You will never see my face and I still win,
I will feel free when I look at the stars,
Our peaceful lives can finally begin.

Chapter 6

A Certain Peace

Difficult Days

The hardest thing I ever had to do,
And you were all there,
I didn't have to say because you already knew,
All you did is care and care.

Myself and my children in a new place,
Afraid to go out, afraid to speak,
Everywhere I looked I saw his face,
I felt drained and very weak.

You told me it was okay to cry,
You told me it was okay to speak,
You believed he was a bad guy,
You told me my future wouldn't be bleak.

I had my ups and my downs,
No matter what, you were always around,
I slowly stopped jumping at all sounds,
I slowly started to put back on my crown.

I fell apart again and again,
You picked me up from the dirt,
You taught me to break away from that chain.
I found a safe haven after all of the hurt.

We talked about the pain I was in,
You helped me feel understood,
You helped me feel comfortable in my own skin,
You made me feel strong and know I am good.

Step by step you told me,
I was stronger than I knew,
In time I would agree,
I would not always feel blue.

The refuge saved my life,
The staff helped me see the light,
They showed me I was more than a beaten housewife,
I no longer live in fight or flight.

The refuge inspired me to help others,
My life has now changed forever,
I want to help the other mothers,
Because of them I will always endeavour.

Time Passes

With time my strength came back,

A new woman I was becoming,

I started to feel back on track,

A new future was forthcoming.

With each passing week,

And every key worker meeting,

You never did critique,

How much I was repeating.

My negative mindset; became less and less,

A hopeful future did replace it,

The refuge helped me progress,

And you never let me quit.

I cried so very many tears,

Everyone's story here is shared,

I shared the hell I lived in for years,

This helped me rid myself of the things I feared.

You helped me feel hopeful,

You told me that I wasn't weak,

That it wasn't me that was a handful,

With each appointment midweek.

With every week that passed,

My strength came back,

I didn't feel like an outcast,

And had less flashbacks.

I know I did the right thing,

For myself and my children,

I am no longer someone's plaything,

And I never will be again.

I am Finally Free

I am free from the pain,

And the sore bruises,

I no longer get the blame,

Or have to hear all his excuses.

I'm in a safe place,

Somewhere out of sight,

I no longer see his face,

Or live in fight or flight.

The other women are just like me,

In need of healing from their past,

In need of a space to feel free,

And not feel like an outcast.

Together, we are a community,

We found a home, somewhere to grow,

Here we have an opportunity,

To really live and learn how to glow.

Bit by bit we learn how to laugh,

And remember how to smile again,

With plenty of help from the staff,

I finally feel like I am sane.

What wonderful people I have met,
They lift me up and make me feel seen,
I no longer feel like I'm under threat,
They make me see that I am a queen.

Life is a Wonder

What do you do when you feel so lost,
When your whole world has changed,
What will this change now cost,
When your whole life has been rearranged.

Just keep breathing, I tell myself,
Step by step, I will figure this out,
Pick up that book from the bookshelf,
Maybe it will help me with my self-doubt.

What can I do when my girls hate school,
Do I tell them it's tough and stick it out,
Or take them to sunbathe by the pool,
Or do we just wait for the burnout.

Life always seems so damn hard,
When things are bad, they get worse,
Is life just one big schoolyard,
Or maybe just a horrible curse.

Sometimes life holds some beauty,
Which helps me to breathe and smile more,
Then I realise I've grown a big booty,
And have dry hands which leave them sore.

Maybe one day I will know my purpose,
Maybe life is just one big circus,
I've experienced pain, love and hardship,
When all we need is companionship.

I try my best which never feels enough,
Then cry over the simplest of stuff,
Why does life feel so damn tough,
Even catching a cold can feel so rough.

I just want to smile and feel happy,
Maybe life isn't as easy as that,
At least I got rid of the one who's snappy,
And I have friends if I need a chat.

I will keep going to see what life has to give,
Fight for the things that I deserve,
I want my girls to be happy and live,
I will sit back and just observe.

One day my life will be for me,
To live everyday happy and carefree,
Have time to enjoy a shopping spree,
And pop into a cafe to drink some tea.

This will probably happen when I'm old and grey,

Have lived my life and finally feel content,

Maybe it will be on my 70th birthday,

And realise I enjoy every laugh, sunrise and scent.

Bluebirds

Every time you meet someone new,
Look in the mirror directly at you,
For this is the person you want to still be,
Even if he, does not agree.

You are amazing, wonderful and true,
Even with everything you have been through,
When someone new comes into your life,
You do not have to become their wife.

Remember everything you have learnt,
If they are everything that you aren't.
Listen to hidden words and their tone,
Lift up your chin and have a backbone.

Assertiveness is the best,
Although we all fall into the rest,
You have the knowledge to set yourself free,
No more crouching down on your knees.

If they make you feel bad or sad,
It builds and builds until you're mad,
Take a step back and remember your training,
This kind of lifestyle is just too draining.

Put your boundaries in place,
Does he accept them with grace,
Or does he cause conflict and second guess you,
And leave you feeling empty and blue.

Does he communicate, is he grateful,
Or is he excessively jealous and hateful,
Does he respect your decisions and lifestyle,
Or is he secretive and very hostile.

Does he take responsibility for his actions,
Or use narcissistic tricks as distractions,
To try and navigate you into his world,
You feel you are in hell and he is in a dreamworld.

Look for someone who fits into your life,
Who does not rush you to be his wife,
Someone who is genuine, caring and kind,
A love that does not leave you feeling blind.

That kind of comfortable that lived in your dreams,
This type of love doesn't tear away at the seams,
A safe space; where you can share your feelings,
Someone who respects your decisions and enjoys the same things.

This kind of love will set you free,
You will feel grounded like a tree,
It will give you peace and freedom,
He will not demand that you feed him.

Look out for those self-serving characteristics,
Trust the statistics and your instincts,
Listen to that voice in your head,
And remember everything that you have read.

You are not in this alone,
Dial the number on your phone,
Help is always out there,
You do not have to rely on your prayers.

www.ingramcontent.com/pod-product-compliance
Lightning Source LLC
Chambersburg PA
CBHW040200100526
44590CB00006B/136